AL•LEONARD
NSTRUMENTAL
PLAY-ALONG

AUDIO ACCESS INCLUDED

PLAYBACK+
ed • Pitch • Balance • Loop

MW00785701

POPULAR HITS

Title	Artist	Page
Breakeven	THE SCRIPT	2
The Climb	MILEY CYRUS	3
Fallin' for You	COLBIE CAILLAT	4
Fireflies	OWL CITY	6
Halo	BEYONCÉ	7
Hey, Soul Sister	TRAIN	8
I Gotta Feeling	THE BLACK EYED PEAS	10
I'm Yours	JASON MRAZ	12
Love Story	TAYLOR SWIFT	14
Need You Now	LADY ANTEBELLUM	16
Poker Face	LADY GAGA	17
Smile	UNCLE KRACKER	18
Use Somebody	KINGS OF LEON	24
Viva La Vida	COLDPLAY	20
You Belong with Me	TAYLOR SWIFT	22

To access audio visit:
www.halleonard.com/mylibrary

Enter Code
4314-6964-7417-3529

ISBN 978-1-61774-004-6

HAL•LEONARD®
7777 W. BLUEMOUND RD. P.O. BOX 13819 MILWAUKEE, WI 53213

BREAKEVEN

VIOLA

Words and Music by STEPHEN KIPNER, ANDREW FRAMPTON,
DANIEL O'DONOGHUE and MARK SHEEHAN

THE CLIMB

from HANNAH MONTANA: THE MOVIE

VIOLA

Words and Music by
JESSI ALEXANDER and JON MABE

FALLIN' FOR YOU

VIOLA

Words and Music by
COLBIE CAILLAT and RICK NOWELS

Moderate Rock

To Coda
mf
D.S. al Coda
CODA
f

FIREFLIES

VIOLA

Words and Music by
ADAM YOUNG

HALO

VIOLA

Words and Music by BEYONCÉ KNOWLES,
RYAN TEDDER and EVAN BOGART

HEY, SOUL SISTER

VIOLA

Words and Music by PAT MONAHAN,
ESPEN LIND and AMUND BJORKLAND

1.
2.
mf
1.
2.
mf
p

I GOTTA FEELING

VIOLA

Words and Music by WILL ADAMS,
ALLAN PINEDA, JAIME GOMEZ, STACY FERGUSON,
DAVID GUETTA and FREDERIC RIESTERER

mf
1.
2.
2

I'M YOURS

VIOLA

Words and Music by
JASON MRAZ

Moderate Reggae

2.
mf
1.
2.
f
1.
2.
2

LOVE STORY

VIOLA

Words and Music by
TAYLOR SWIFT

mf
mp
f

NEED YOU NOW

VIOLA

Words and Music by HILLARY SCOTT,
CHARLES KELLEY, DAVE HAYWOOD and JOSH KEAR

POKER FACE

VIOLA

Words and Music by
STEFANI GERMANOTTA and REDONE

SMILE

VIOLA

Words and Music by BLAIR DALY, JEREMY BOSE,
MATTHEW SHAFER and JOHN HARDING

1.
3
2.
mf
mf
f
1., 2.
3.
2
mf

VIVA LA VIDA

VIOLA

Words and Music by GUY BERRYMAN,
JON BUCKLAND, WILL CHAMPION and CHRIS MARTIN

1.
3
2.
mf
1.
2.

YOU BELONG WITH ME

VIOLA

Words and Music by
TAYLOR SWIFT and LIZ ROSE

2.
1.
2.
mp
f

USE SOMEBODY

VIOLA

Words and Music by CALEB FOLLOWILL, NATHAN FOLLOWILL,
JARED FOLLOWILL and MATTHEW FOLLOWILL